CENGAGE Learning

Drama for Students, Volume 12

Staff

Editor: Elizabeth Thomason.

Contributing Editors: Anne Marie Hacht, Michael L. LaBlanc, Ira Mark Milne, Jennifer Smith.

Managing Editor: Dwayne D. Hayes.

Research: Victoria B. Cariappa, *Research Manager*. Cheryl Warnock, *Research Specialist*. Tamara Nott, Tracie A. Richardson, *Research Associates*. Nicodemus Ford, Sarah Genik, Timothy Lehnerer, Ron Morelli, *Research Assistants*.

Permissions: Maria Franklin, *Permissions Manager*. Debra J. Freitas, Jacqueline Jones, Julie Juengling, *Permissions Assistants*.

Manufacturing: Mary Beth Trimper, *Manager, Composition and Electronic Prepress*. Evi Seoud, *Assistant Manager, Composition Purchasing and Electronic Prepress*. Stacy Melson, *Buyer*.

Imaging and Multimedia Content Team: Barbara Yarrow, *Manager*. Randy Bassett, *Imaging Supervisor*. Robert Duncan, Dan Newell, *Imaging Specialists*. Pamela A. Reed, *Imaging Coordinator*. Leitha Etheridge-Sims, Mary Grimes, David G. Oblender, *Image Catalogers*. Robyn V. Young, *Project Manager*. Dean Dauphinais, *Senior Image Editor*. Kelly A. Quin, *Image Editor*.

Product Design Team: Kenn Zorn, *Product Design Manager*. Pamela A. E. Galbreath, *Senior Art Director*. Michael Logusz, *Graphic Artist*.

Copyright ©2001
Gale Group, Inc.
27500 Drake Road
Farmington Hills, MI 48331-3535

ISBN 0-7876-4086-7
ISSN 1094-9232

Printed in the United States of America.
10 9 8 7 6 5 4 3 2 1

The Seagull

Anton Chekhov

1896

Introduction

Anton Chekhov's *Chayka* or *The Seagull* (variously translated in English as *The Sea Gull* and *The Sea-Gull*) is the first play in the author's second period of writing for the theater—that of the last few years of his life—in which he penned his widely acknowledged dramatic masterpieces. With it, after a hiatus of seven years, Chekhov again returned to writing plays, and he revealed his mastery of techniques that he would exploit in his other great plays of that final period: *Uncle Vanya, Three Sisters,* and *The Cherry Orchard.* In all of them, Chekhov employs a method of "indirect action," one in which characters confront changes that result from offstage occurrences, often in a period of the characters' lives that elapses between acts. The plays also share the unique Chekhovian mood, a pervasive melancholic tone that arises from the haplessness of the characters that seem destined either to wallow in self-pity or indifference or consume themselves in frustrated passion. It is in these plays, with his special brand of "slice of life" realism, that Chekhov journeys to the outer limits of comedy, to a point in which its distinctness from quasi-tragic *drame* is blurred and at some points all but lost.

In *The Seagull,* a work that the author himself claimed contained "five tons of love," is a play about a very human tendency to reject love that is freely given and seek it where it is withheld. Many of its characters are caught in a destructive, triangular relationship that evokes both pathos and humor. What the characters cannot successfully parry is the destructive force of time, the passage of which robs some, like Madame Arkadina, of beauty, and others, like her son Konstantine, of hope.

When the play was first staged, in St. Petersburg in 1896, it was very badly received. The audience was unwilling to applaud or even abide a work that in technique and style countered the traditional kind of play built on comfortable conventions. Audiences were simply not ready to accept a work that seemed to violate almost all dramatic conventions, a play that, for example, had no clear protagonist or an easily identified moral conflict or characters who rigorously kept to points relevant to that conflict in their dialogue. For Chekhov, the response was devastating. There seemed to be no audience prepared to welcome the "new forms" championed by one of the play's characters, the young writer Konstantine Treplyov.

Had Chekhov's friend, Nemirovich-Danchenko, not taken an interest in the work despite its initial stage failure, the dramatist might well have given up writing for the theater. Nemirovich-Danchenko and his more famous codirector of the famous Moscow Art Theatre, Konstantin Stanislavsky, brought *The Seagull* to the stage again in 1898 and turned it into a remarkable success, the first Chekhov play that they produced in what soon became one of the most fortuitous associations in the history of modern drama. It was their staging of *The Seagull* and the other later plays of Chekhov that brought the writer his lasting acclaim as a dramatist.

Author Biography

Anton Chekhov was born on January 17, 1860, in Taganrog, a dreary Russian seaport village on the Black Sea. His grandfather was an emancipated serf who had managed to buy his own freedom. His father, Pravel Yegorovitch Chekhov, a cruel and dictatorial taskmaster who made his children's lives miserable, ran a small grocery store. In 1876, that business failed, forcing the family to flee to the anonymity of Moscow to escape from creditors. Although Chekhov's fame as a dramatist rests largely on works he wrote during the last eight years of his life, his love of the theater extended back into his youth in Taganrog, where he frequented dramatic presentations at that city's provincial playhouses. Young Anton remained in Taganrog to complete his schooling before following the family to Moscow and entering that city's university to study medicine.

It was there that Chekhov began writing his sketches and stories, works that fairly quickly brought him financial independence and a moderate degree of fame. Between 1880, when the first of his pieces appeared, and 1887, Chekhov published about 600 pieces in periodicals. Quite literally, he wrote his humorous sketches as "potboilers," works providing money enough for his family to get back on its feet.

By 1884, when he graduated from the

university and began practicing medicine, Chekhov already knew that he had contracted tuberculosis, a disease that would leave him but twenty additional years to write. His success and much improved financial situation soon allowed him to give up medicine to concentrate on his writing, though he sometimes worked as a physician to help the poor.

At first Chekhov did not take his writing very seriously, but starting in 1885, after he moved to St. Petersburg, his attitude began to change. He became a close friend of A. S. Suvorin, the editor of *Novoe vremja,* a fairly conservative journal. Recognizing Chekhov's genius, Suvorin encouraged the writer to take more pride in his work and to seek a greater critical reputation. It was there, too, that Chekhov fell under the influence of the great novelist, Leo Tolstoy, especially that writer's moral preachments, including his passive response to evil.

Chekov began to write plays at about the same time that he started writing fiction but did not immediately achieve the success and acclaim that he did in fiction. His work in drama falls into two distinct periods. The first, from 1881 until 1895, is predominately one in which he wrote adaptations of his prose sketches as curtain-raisers or "vaudevilles," single-act farces of the sort that were immensely popular in Russian theater at the time. Two of these pieces, *The Bear* (also known as *The Brute* and *The Boar*) and *The Marriage Proposal,* are extremely durable examples of this kind. Chekhov also experimented with longer pieces in his early years, but, except in the case of *Ivanov*

(1887), he had little success with them. In fact, because one of them, *The Wood Demon* (1889), was so chillingly received by critics and was rejected for performance, Chekhov all but gave up writing drama for the next seven years. With *The Seagull* (1896), he entered his second period of dramatic writing and produced the world-renowned masterpieces on which his fame as playwright largely rests. In this second period, lasting to his death in 1904, he wrote his greatest plays, which, besides *The Seagull,* include *Uncle Vanya* (1899), *The Cherry Orchard* (1900), and *Three Sisters* (1901). It was also in this period that Chekhov commenced his fortuitous association with the Moscow Art Theater, then under the joint directorship of Constantin Stanislavsky and Chekhov's friend, Vladimir Nemirovich-Danchenko. In their stage interpretation of his work, these two men and their actors brought the author both great fame and fortune. His sickness soon took its toll, however, and after his marriage to the actress Olga Knipper in 1901 until his death in 1904, Chekhov's failing health depleted his energy and prevented him from adding new works to his limited dramatic canon.

However, by 1901 he had done enough to acquire an international reputation. In these latter plays, Chekhov perfected hallmark techniques and a style that earned him a lasting reputation as a seminal figure in modern drama—in the minds of many the coequal of the "father" of modern drama, Henrik Ibsen. To this day, in manner and technique, he is still admired and imitated by aspiring playwrights.

Plot Summary

Act 1

The Seagull opens on an early summer evening in a park on the estate of Peter Nikolaevich Sorin, brother to Irina Arkadina, a celebrated actress. A small stage blocks a view of the lake that borders the park. Around it are some bushes, a few chairs, and a table. Behind the platform's curtain, Yakov and other laborers are finishing work on the makeshift structure.

Masha and Semyon Medvedenko are returning from a walk. She is the daughter of Sorin's steward, Ilya Shamreyeff. He is a poor schoolmaster, infatuated with her but perplexed by her sorrow, which is overtly revealed in her mournful world view and black clothing. He cannot understand why she is sad, for she is not poor. From their conversation, it is learned that a play written by Konstantine, Madame Treplyov's son, is about to be performed, and that he and Nina Zaryechny, who is to act in it, are in love.

As Masha tries to discourage Semyon's love, Sorin and Konstantine Treplyov enter. Sorin confides that the country does not really suit him. He complains to Masha about the dog that her father keeps chained up, but she curtly dismisses his request that she tell Shamreyeff that the dog's howling bothers Sorin. She and Medvedenko exit, followed by Yakov and the other workers who go off for a swim while Sorin and Treplyov await the appearance of Nina. Sorin, after remarking on his own frumpishness and inadequacies as a lover, asks the cause of Treplyov's mother's bad humor. Konstantine claims that she is jealous and launches into a diatribe about her inadequacies—her petulance, stinginess, volatile temperament, and, the greatest shortcoming of all, her shallow view of the theater. He then explains that with "new forms" he is helping to sweep away the old, worn-out tradition. He also reveals that he is in fact very jealous of her, of her fame and her lover, the novelist Boris Trigorin, who annoys him because of his success.

Konstantine's assessment of Trigorin is interrupted by the arrival of Nina, upon whom he clearly fawns. Nina, concerned that she might be late, explains that she has had to slip away from her father and stepmother, who do not approve of their "Bohemian" neighbors. She is obviously very nervous, and after Sorin goes off to collect his other guests for the play's performance, she explains that she is fearful of acting before such a literary luminary as Boris Trigorin, whose stories she admires. She then complains to Konstantine that his play has no "living characters in it," offending him.

The others begin arriving, starting with Pauline, wife of Ilya Shamreyeff, and Eugene Dorn, a doctor. They discuss Dorn's enchantment with Nina and his easy success with women, something that has prompted her jealousy and suggests that they are engaged in an illicit affair. Their talk is cut off by the arrival of the others—Madame Arkadina, Sorin, Trigorin, Shamreyeff, Medvedenko, and Masha. They are discussing the state of the Russian theater and its actors, the "mighty oaks" that in Shamreyeff's view are now nothing but "stumps." After Irina asks Konstantine about his play and exchanges lines with him from Shakespeare's *Hamlet,* the performance begins. It consists of a recitation by Nina, a prospective glance 200,000 years into the future, when most life forms of our era will long since have become extinct. It is more a threnody than a play. When the spirit represented by Nina is approached by the Devil, represented by two red "eyes" and the smell of sulphur, Irina begins laughing, greatly annoying her son, who orders the curtain closed, aborting Nina's performance, and storms off in disgust. His mother is upbraided by Sorin, who seems much more aware of her son's hurt pride than she is. She finds him simply "an unruly, conceited boy," one whose ideas about theater arise from his temperament, not from any artistic convictions. She soon relents, however, and expresses regrets for hurting his feelings.

When Nina appears from behind the stage, Madame Arkadina praises her for her voice and looks, and Nina confides that she has hopes of becoming an actress. Irina introduces her to Trigorin. They briefly discuss the play, the substance of which seems to have evaded them. He then talks of his joy in fishing, a pleasure that surprises Nina. The act winds down with some final revelations that help explain the character tensions in the play. Nina, afraid of her father, must run off, but it is clear that her regret at leaving arises from her infatuation with Trigorin. After she leaves, Madame Arkadina explains the girl's unfortunate situation as the daughter of a man who has taken a second wife. She then goes off with Sorin, who complains about the damp night air. Dorn is left alone, but is soon joined by Konstantine Treplyov, who complains of being pursued by Masha, an "unbearable creature." Dorn praises him for his play of "abstract ideas," of which he approves. Treplyov, almost frantic, is merely interested in finding Nina, and quickly runs off just after Masha enters. After his departure, treating Dorn like a surrogate father, she asks for his help. She is tortured by her love for Konstantine. Dorn remarks then on the nervousness of everyone and the "magic lake" that seems to have inspired the hapless love of all of them.

Act 2

The action continues on another part of Sorin's estate, a croquet lawn near the lake. It is noon on a hot day, perhaps a week later. Seated on a tree-shaded bench, Madame Arkadina and Masha engage in idle conversation while Dorn attempts to read a de Maupassant story. Rather vainly, Irina asks Dorn to say which of them, herself or Masha, looks the youngest, then carries on about her fine appearance and flawless grooming. She exclaims that she never looks frumpy, an obvious contrast to her brother, Sorin. She takes the book from Dorn and reads aloud, then, apropos of the author's words, comments on her relationship with Trigorin.

When Sorin enters, accompanied by Nina and Medvedenko, who bring in his wheel chair, the conversation turns to Trigorin and his persistent habit of fishing alone and then to Konstantine, who Madame Arkadina finds "sad and morose." While Sorin snores in his wheel chair, Masha effusively praises Konstantine's genius and poetic soul. Annoyed, Irina wakes her brother and complains about his failure to take medicine. Dorn, in turn, carps about Sorin's consumption of wine and his smoking. According to the doctor, these habits affect his character, but Sorin only laughs and defends his use of sherry and cigars as a defense against his boring life, which in turn prompts a discourse by his sister on the dullness of country living.

After Shamreyeff and Pauline enter, and Irina confirms that she had hoped to take a horse and carriage to town in the afternoon, the steward grows angry and abrasive over her request. She threatens to leave for Moscow, and he threatens to quit his post. Followed by Trigorin, she exits with a complaint about the insults she is subjected to at Sorin's estate, leaving her brother to rebuke his steward for his insolence. Thereafter all go off except Dorn and Pauline. The doctor claims that Sorin should fire her husband but says that it will not happen, that instead the steward will be pardoned for his rudeness. Pauline begins complaining about her husband's coarseness, then pleads with Dorn to requite her love. She grows contrite when rebuffed, admitting her jealousy of other women.

Nina, who has been picking flowers, joins them and explains that Irina is inside crying and that her brother is in the throes of an asthma attack. She gives Dorn the flowers, but as he goes in to tend to Sorin, Pauline demands them from him. She tears them to pieces and throws them away before following him into the house. Alone, Nina expostulates on the strangeness of seeing a famous actress grow so passionate over nothing at all. She is joined by Konstantine Treplyov who carries a gun and a dead seagull, which he lays at her feet. He claims that is the way that he will end his life. Irritated, she complains that he cannot speak except in symbols. He complains bitterly about her growing frigidity towards him. When Trigorin appears, Konstantine remarks that he will not stand in Nina's way and exits.

Alone with the novelist, Nina talks of her envy for his fame, something that he claims he is unresponsive towards. She argues that his life is beautiful, but he rejoins that his writing is an annoying obsession that is more punishing than rewarding. The act of writing may be pleasurable, he says, but he detests the result. As a writer, he exclaims, he hates himself, for other than as a "landscape artist" he is "false" to the very core of his being. Nina is not discouraged, however, and expresses her willingness to sacrifice anything for fame.

After Madame Arkadina calls him from the

house, Trigorin is about to go in when he notices the dead seagull and asks Nina about it. He then asks her to try to persuade Irina to stay and makes a note in a book that he carries with him. He is jotting down ideas for a sad story about a girl much like Nina, who a man destroys like the seagull. Madame Arkadina, appearing at a window in the house, calls again, announcing that they are staying after all. After Trigorin goes in, the act ends with Nina's remark that "it's all a dream!"

Act 3

The scene shifts now to the interior of Sorin's house, to the dining room. From the conversation, it is made clear that about a week has elapsed since Konstantine shot the seagull. From the trunk and hat boxes deposited on the floor, it is also clear that preparations for a departure are in progress.

Masha is alone with Trigorin, who sits at a table eating his lunch. She tells him that she is going to marry Medvedenko, even though she does not love him. The fact that she is drinking annoys the writer. He is also upset because Treplyov has been behaving badly. As Boris explains, during the elapsed period between the acts, Konstantine has bungled an attempt to kill himself with a pistol shot to the head. He is reportedly also planning to challenge the novelist to a duel and has been preaching about the need for new art forms, which Boris finds offensively inflexible. As Nina enters, Masha speaks of Medvedenko as a poor and not very clever man, but one who loves her. She plans to marry him from pity as much as anything else.

After she exits, Nina gives Boris a medal that she has had engraved to commemorate their meeting. He recalls the moment when he saw her in her white dress with the seagull lying at her feet. They are then interrupted by Madame Arkadina and Sorin, who enter followed by Yakov, who is packing for Trigorin and Irina. The novelist goes off to find one of his books, lines from which are referenced on the medal's inscription.

Madame Arkadina tells Sorin to look after Konstantine, whom she is leaving behind. She says that she will never understand her son's bungled suicide attempt but that she must take Trigorin away because of Treplyov's threats. Sorin says that her son's behavior springs from his wounded pride and that she could help him by giving him some money for clothes, making him feel less like a poor relation. At first, Irina insists that she has none to give Konstantine, but she finally confesses that she has some money but that, as an actress, she needs it for her costumes.

When Sorin begins to stagger, about to faint, Madame Arkadina cries out for help. Both Treplyov and Medvedenko enter to assist, but the spell quickly passes, and Sorin again insists that he will accompany Irina and Boris to town. He goes off with Medvedenko, who poses the riddle of the Sphinx to him as they leave.

Alone with his mother, Treplyov asks her to

change the bandage on his head, after first suggesting that she should lend her brother, Sorin, some money. When she is done applying the fresh bandage, Konstantine asks why she continues to be influenced by Trigorin, who, he says, is a coward for running off to escape a duel with him. A heated argument ensues over the novelist, as Konstantine attacks both Boris and his writings, and Irina defends him. She accuses her son of envy, and he explodes, announcing that his talent is greater than that of both his mother and Trigorin put together. In angry recriminations, he calls her a miser, while she retorts that he is a beggar. A sudden, contrite reconciliation follows, as Konstantine confides that he has lost the love of Nina, leaving him spiritually impoverished.

Just as Irina exacts a promise from Konstantine to make up with Trigorin, the writer enters and Treplyov hastily retreats from the room. Thereafter, the writer confesses his feelings for Nina, asking that they stay a bit longer. He pleads with Irina to let him go, to free him from her influence. She grows angry, then weepy, and finally throws herself on her knees pleading with him to remain true to her. She grows very possessive, overbearing his weak will and exacting a promise from him not to leave her. Then, as if nothing had just happened, she says that he can stay on for another week if he wishes.

Sorin's steward, Shamreyeff, enters to announce that the horse and carriage are ready for the trip into town, a notice he embellishes with recollections of an unintended comic moment in a serious melodrama. The family retainers begin scurrying in and out with the luggage and clothes, as Sorin, Pauline, and Medvedenko enter. Gifts are given, after which Sorin goes off to get in the carriage, followed by the others. Nina then enters, encountering Trigorin, who has returned to find his walking stick. As the act closes, the pair have a passionate moment in which they promise to meet in Moscow and seal the promise with an ardent kiss.

Act 4

The action again occurs in Sorin's estate house, in one of his drawing rooms that has been put to use by Treplyov as a study. It is stormy night, a full two years later. At rise, Masha and Medvedenko, now her husband, enter, looking for Konstantine, who, it is soon learned, has become a moderately successful writer. For the moment or so that the couple are alone, they reveal that they have a child, on whom Medvedenko dotes but towards whom Masha seems completely indifferent. The baby and her husband seem merely to annoy her.

They are joined by Treplyov and Pauline, who come in carrying bedding for turning a sofa into a bed for Sorin's use. The old man, now ill, has insisted on being near Konstantine. Medvedenko then leaves, ignored by Masha and rather curtly dismissed by Pauline, who thereafter turns warmer attention to Konstantine, affectionately running her hand through his hair as she discusses his unanticipated acclaim as an author and begs him to be kind to Masha. Without uttering a word, he rises from his desk and exits, leaving Pauline and Masha to discuss Masha's forlorn love for him. Masha's only hope is that her husband's imminent transfer will put her ache behind her.

After Konstantine begins playing a melancholy waltz in another room, Dorn and Medvedenko enter, pushing Sorin in his wheelchair and arguing about money, a constant problem for the school teacher. Dorn says that he has no money either, claiming that his life savings have been spent on a journey abroad. As the rest converse with Sorin, it is learned that Madame Arkadina has gone to town to meet Trigorin, prompting Sorin to remark on his own illness and Dorn's unwillingness to let him have any medicine. Sorin wishes to give Konstantine matter for a story, a thinly-veiled, abstract account of his own life, prompting Dorn to remark on the old man's self pity and the fear of death.

Treplyov returns and sits by his uncle just as Medvedenko begins asking Dorn about his travels. After identifying Genoa as his favorite foreign city, Dorn inquires after Nina. Treplyov gives an account of her poor fortune as both an actress and Trigorin's mistress. He notes that in letters that she exchanged with Konstantine, Nina always signed herself "the seagull," and that though she did not complain in them, he could sense the sadness behind her words. He also reveals that she is now in town, staying at an inn, and that her father and stepmother have disowned her.

When Madame Arkadina and Trigorin arrive, accompanied by Shamreyeff, and greetings are exchanged, Trigorin graciously remarks on Treplyov's newly acquired fame as a writer and announces his intention to return to Moscow the next day, after fishing on the lake in the morning. Masha asks Shamreyeff to lend a horse to her husband, a request that prompts the steward to mimic her and Medvedenko to insist that he can walk home. Most of the characters sit down to play lotto, but Treplyov leaves after looking through a magazine given to him by Trigorin and announcing that Boris had read his own but not Treplyov's story. He once again begins playing the sad waltz offstage. The ensuing conversation of those remaining is interspersed with exclamations relating to the game. During it, Irina talks of her ongoing successes as an actress, while Trigorin voices doubts about Konstantine's skills as a writer. Dorn in turn defends Treplyov's artistry, while Madame Arkadina confesses that she had not even read any of her son's work.

Treplyov stops playing and returns to the drawing room as Shamreyeff informs Boris Trigorin that he has had the seagull stuffed for him. When Trigorin wins the lotto game, all the characters except Treplyov go off for some supper. In a monologue, Treplyov remarks that, despite his preaching about new forms, his work is becoming as routine as that which he despises. Then, hearing a tap at the window, he opens the doors, goes out, and leads Nina into the room. After she talks morosely of her faltering career, and her disappointments,

Treplyov reveals his ambivalent feelings towards her, his love-hate, from which she recoils and tries to distance herself. She starts to try to leave, but Konstantine pleads with her to stay. She verges on going when she overhears Madame Arkadina and Trigorin in another room, and she reveals that, despite Boris' wretched treatment of her, she still loves him. She embraces Treplyov, then runs out through the terrace door. Left behind, Konstantine tears up all his manuscripts, then exits through another door.

After Dorn enters and moves a chair that Treplyov had used to block a door, he is joined by Irina and Pauline, and then Masha, Shamreyeff and Trigorin, who have returned to resume their game. Yakov follows with a tray and bottles. Almost immediately, they hear a shot from offstage. Dorn goes out to see what has happened, then returns. He exclaims that a bottle of ether in his bag exploded but then leads Trigorin away from the rest and, in a lowered voice, tells him to take Irina away, explaining, at the curtain, that Konstantine has shot himself again and that this time, presumably, has killed himself, though Trigorin does not explicitly say so.

Pauline Andreevna

Ilya Shamreyeff's wife, Pauline is often found in the company of the physician, Eugene Dorn, with whom she may be carrying on an illicit love affair, though whether her passion for him is being requited or is merely expressed remains one of the play's mysteries. In any case, she is seeking fulfillment outside of her marriage. Dorn, who has always been popular with the opposite sex, seems noncommittal in their relationship, even bored by it. She, meanwhile, is well aware of the deadening effect that time is likely to have on her hopes and tries to push him into running off with her. He seems completely disinterested, however, worn down by his weary life as a physician. He is virtually penniless and no longer feels the stirring of passion, thus nothing really ever comes of their relationship.

Madame Irina Nikolaevna Arkadina

See Madame Treplyov.

Eugene Sergeevich Dorn

Dorn is a doctor, like Chekhov himself, and as

such is a familiar figure in the playwright's dramas. He is a rather world-weary man, seemingly indifferent to his calling. After years of practicing medicine, he is virtually penniless, having spent his life's earnings on foreign travel. As if resentful towards his profession, he seems almost unwilling any longer to attempt to help the sick, notably Sorin.

Like some men, Dorn in his life has had no trouble attracting the interest of the opposite sex, and in this fact he contrasts with Sorin who complains that he has had no luck at all with women. The doctor is ardently pursued by Pauline, Shamreyeff's wife, but he resists her efforts to get him to run off with her. He does not openly repel her love but instead waits for time to wear it away.

Curiously enough, only Dorn gets excited over Konstantine's work, first his play and then his fiction, about which he is most effusive in his praise. He shares Treplyov's belief that something like a literature of "new forms" is needed to sweep out the old.

Maria Ilyinishna

See Masha.

Kostya

See Konstantine Gavrilovich Treplyov.

Masha

Daughter of Ilya and Pauline Shamreyeff, Masha (also called Maria Ilyinishna) is a young woman who assumes a melancholic demeanor, though it may be more fashionable than real. She dresses in mourning black, the outward reflection of her inner sorrow—or at least that is what she tells Medvedenko, the schoolmaster who dotes on her. She seems to luxuriate in his misery, however, and her posturing borders on the ridiculous.

Media Adaptations

- In 1968, *The Seagull* was adapted to film by director Sidney Lumet. Its stellar casts includes James Mason as Trigorin, Alfred Lynch as Medvedenko, Ronald Radd as Shamraev, Vanessa Redgrave as Nina, Simone Signoret as Arkadina,

David Warner as Konstantin, Harry Andrews as Sorin, Eileen Herlie as Polina (Pauline), Kathleen Widdoes as Masha, and Denholm Elliot as Dorn. It is available on video from Warner Brothers.

- A Russian film version of *The Seagull* was produced in 1971, directed by Yuri Karasik and featuring Alla Demidova, Vladimir Chetverikov, Nikolai Plotnikov, Lyudmila Savelyeva, Valentina Telichkina, Yuri Yakovlev, Yefim Kopelyan, Armen Dzhigarkhanyan, Sofiya Pavlova, Sergei Torkachevsky, S. Smirnov, and Genrikas Kurauskas. It is available from Facets Multimedia, Inc., with English subtitles.

- *The Seagull* was produced for television, both in the United States and in Europe. In 1968, the year Lumet's film was made, a British version of the work was produced as a "Play of the Month" selection, featuring Robert Stephens. In 1975, the play was produced on American television, and featured, among others, Blythe Danner as Nina, Olympia Dukakis as Polina, Lee Grant as Irina Arkadina, and Frank Langella as Treplev (Treplyov).

Three years later, another British version was aired, with a cast headed by Michael Gambon. There is also an Italian version, directed by Marco Bellocchio, dating from 1977. Also aired in the United States, this version featured Laura Betti, Giulio Brogi, Remo Girone, and Pamela Villoresi. While these performances attest to the great resurgence of interest in the plays of Chekhov, tapes of them have never been released for commercial use.

Masha's problem is her unrequited love for Konstantine Treplyov, who seems utterly blind to her desire and considers her a pest. He is in love with Nina and has his own problems with unrequited love. Although Masha does not love Medvedenko, who is a rather bland and unimaginative fellow, she ends up marrying him. They have a child, towards whom she reveals not the slightest maternal interest. She is ill tempered and cold towards her well-meaning husband, as is her mother, Pauline, who has been privy to Masha's hopes for a love liaison with Treplyov. At the last, she can only hope that her dull husband will be assigned to a new district so that she might put her painful love for Konstantine behind her.

Semyon Semyonovich Medvedenko

A rather unassuming and placid schoolmaster, Medvedenko diligently woos Masha, a woman whose passionate nature and eccentric manner simply seem puzzling to him. Because his own needs are so mundane and simple, he is unable to understand why she is so sad. As he observes, unlike him, she is hardly lacking in creature comforts. That her sorrow might spring from a despised love or some other nonmaterial cause simply escapes his understanding or sympathy.

Though she does not love or admire Medvedenko, Masha marries him, then behaves badly towards both him and their child. Medvedenko suffers her abuse without complaint, unwilling, perhaps, to risk the loss of her.

Ilya Afanasevich Shamreyeff

Ilya Shamreyeff, a retired army lieutenant, is Peter Sorin's irascible and tyrannical steward. As the inept Sorin complains, Ilya runs the estate, which, in truth, Sorin permits because rural life bores him. Peter is content to let Shamreyeff take charge, though the man is rather insolent and moody. At times he is also rude to Sorin's guests, especially when he feels put upon. He seems to resent the fact that he is a retainer and not their social equal.

Ilya is married to Pauline, and Masha is their daughter. He seldom seems to be in their company, busy as he is sorting out such matters as how the horses are to be used at any particular moment. He seems blissfully unaware of his wife's infatuation with the physician, Eugene Dorn, and indifferent towards his daughter, who complains that she is unable to talk to him. With her, he seems much more gruff and short-tempered than loving. He has, in fact, some of the insularity that is characteristic of many career military men, and he has clearly alienated both his wife and daughter.

In a few instances, Shamreyeff talks at length about the theater, recalling what he considers great moments in Russian stage history. His nostalgia for the low comedy that was part of the traditional theater offers a contrast with Treplyov's attack upon traditional works as cliche ridden and formulaic.

Peter Nikolaevich Sorin

Peter Sorin, brother to Madame Arkadina, is a retired magistrate in his early sixties. He is also the host and owner of the country estate that is the play's setting.

Although easy-going and genial, Sorin constantly complains about the tedium of country living. He thinks of himself as a man of the town, miscast in his retirement role as rural squire. There is about him the smell of mortality, and in the course of the play he seems to wither away as his sense of boredom saps his energy. Towards the end of the play, he is confined to a wheel chair where he dozes and snores as life continues around him. Once an important man and the embodiment of authority, he can no longer curb the insubordination of his estate steward, Shamreyeff, or even of ordinary workmen. He has trouble with others as well, the physician Dorn, for example, who seems unwilling to heed his request for medicine. Towards him and other guests, Sorin seem pathetically deferential.

However, as a critic of Madame Arkadina's treatment of her son Konstantine, Sorin points up important character flaws in his sister, confirming, for example, the selfishness of which Treplyov accuses his mother, but she does not change one iota as a result of his criticism. He does love his nephew and provides him with a home and place to work, revealing a greater sense of concern for his welfare than Konstantine's mother has. Yet Sorin's fatherly love for his nephew is not powerful enough to stay the suicidal impulses of the young writer.

Konstantine Gavrilovich Treplyov

Son to Madame Arkadina and nephew to Peter Sorin, Konstantine Treplyov (also known as Kostya) is an aspiring writer in his early twenties. Moody and often depressed, Treplyov has an antagonistic relationship with his mother. He is an unrelenting critic of the traditional theater, which he considers tired and moribund, while she, having made her successful career in that theater, defends it. It is she who interrupts the performance of his "new forms" play on Sorin's estate, mocking its special effects and enraging her son, a signal event that sets in motion the destructive recriminations that further erode the relationship of Konstantine and his mother.

Treplyov's play also manages to alienate Nina Zaryechny, who, although she acts in the play, neither likes it nor understands what it is all about. Although Treplyov loves her, she turns away from him, attracted to the novelist Boris Trigorin and sets out to become an actress. From jealousy and envy, Treplyov verbally attacks Trigorin as a coward and wants to challenge him to duel. He also tries to kill himself, though the effort is suspect because, although he is able to bring down a seagull with a rifle shot, he bungles at least one try at blowing his brains out with a pistol.

In the final part of the play, despite his growing success as a writer, Treplyov remains melancholy and alienated from the other characters. He becomes critical of his own work, observing that it is becoming as conventional as the literature he had attacked for being staid and worn out. At the last, realizing that Nina will never relinquish her love for Boris and profoundly depressed by his own sense of his inadequacies, he makes a second and probably successful attempt on his life.

Madame Treplyov

Madame Treplyov (also called Irina Nikolaevna Arkadina) is the sister of Peter Sorin and mother of Konstantine Treplyov. She is a very successful and once a strikingly beautiful actress, who, although in her mid forties, still looks much younger, a fact in which she takes great pride.

Although a sentimental woman prone to effusive emotional moments, she is a poor parent, stingy with her money and totally disinclined to sacrifice anything for her son. She is, in fact, rather embarrassed around him, in large measure because his presence serves to remind her of her real age. Although she is capable of tender moments with him, there is a strong antagonism between them that may be interpreted as having Oedipal undercurrents. In some of their exchanges, recriminations fly back and forth between them, and from start to finish she remains more hostile than loving towards him. Her antagonism is a major reason for his attempts at suicide.

Madame Treplyov holds the writer Boris Trigorin, her lover, under her spell, and although he is drawn to Nina Zaryechny, he ends up treating her badly and returning to Irina, who at one point plays shamelessly with his emotions and loyalty. Irina's son despises Trigorin, both for his writing and his apparent lack of courage. Irina is not able to make peace between them, though she hardly seems to try very hard. Because she is so selfish and self-centered, she cannot understand her son, and is simply mystified by his attack on the theatrical tradition in which she has won her fame and fortune. More often than not, she finds her son to be gloomy and depressing, an unfit companion. Still, she is fond of her brother, Sorin, though her concern for his failing health hardly matches her concern with her own fading beauty.

Boris Alexeevich Trigorin

Boris Trigorin, a successful novelist, is the traveling companion and lover of Irina Arkadina. His relationship with her and the acclaim accorded his art gnaw at Konstantine's innards. He holds the older man in contempt, as much from envy and jealousy as any really contemptible character flaws in Boris. The conflict between the two provides a good part of the play's tension.

Trigorin is actually a rather easy-going fellow. His success has made him neither arrogant nor aloof; thus, despite his wretched treatment of Nina, he remains rather likable as a character. His favorite activity at Sorin's estate is fishing in the "magical" lake, something that gives him peace and contentment.

Trigorin's fiction, realistic in nature, also rankles Konstantine, who is preaching a new style and mode in literature. Trigorin is open to new styles, and sees no reason why Treplyov's writing cannot coexist with his own. Konstantine is not so obliging, however, and seems bent on destroying both the man and his work. A central irony of the play is that Trigorin, without even trying, wins the adoration of Nina with whom Treplyov is hopelessly in love.

Yakov

Other than the steward, Ilya Shamreyeff, Yakov is the only named employee on Sorin's estate. He is one of the workers who at the opening of the play are putting the finishing touches on the stage being built for Konstantine's play, but later he also appears as a household servant, helping with the visitors' luggage and serving drinks. Like the unnamed cook and housemaids, he is otherwise an anonymous character.

Nina Mikhailovna Zaryechny

Nina Zaryechny is the pretty daughter of a wealthy landowner living on an estate near Sorin's estate. Her tyrannical father and stepmother disapprove of the "bohemian" guests of Sorin and try to prevent her involvement with them, but she is too much a free spirit to bend to their will. At first she seems to be in love with Konstantine, but after her performance in his play is interrupted, her loyalty to him quickly wanes. She is rather star struck by Trigorin, a much older man emotionally attached to Irina Arkadina. However, in her he sees a story, drawing parallels to her and the seagull that Treplyov has shot and laid at her feet. When she sets out to make a career of acting, somewhat precipitously encouraged by Irina, she takes up with Trigorin and bears his child. Irina's encouragement is somewhat suspect, for in some ways, like Konstantine, Nina is Irina's nemesis, representing as she does the youth and beauty that in Irina is swiftly fading. In any case, Nina's relationship with Trigorin is ill fated. He abandons her and the baby soon dies. However, despite Trigorin's rather wretched treatment of her, Nina cannot abandon her love for him, even though she has no more realistic hopes as a result of disappointments in love, the loss of her child, and her faltering acting career. The fact that she will not renew her earlier love relationship with Konstantine takes its final emotional toll on the young man, who, at the end of play, again shoots himself.

Themes

If there is an overriding theme in *The Seagull,* it is that humankind's greatest enemy is time, the relentless enemy of passion and hope. It is a play of hopelessly misplaced love or desire. Many of the characters want love from others who are either indifferent or have emotional commitments elsewhere and are frustrated in their own turn. There are no fortuitous liaisons in the play. Rather, except for the residual and somewhat enigmatic passion that binds Irina Arkadina and Boris Trigorin, the passions of each of the needful characters make them miserable, albeit, at times, comically so.

Topics for Further Study

- Investigate Henrik Ibsen's use of symbolism in *The Wild Duck* and compare it to Chekhov's use of it in *The Seagull*.

- Investigate life expectancy and infant mortality rates in Russia at the time of Chekhov's play and relate your findings to two significant revelations of *The Seagull,* the death of Nina's child and Sorin's disclosed age.

- Research the state of medicine in Russia in the 1890s and relate your findings to Dorn, the physician in *The Seagull,* and to Chekhov's own medical career and struggle with tuberculosis.

- Study some of the artistic manifestos of the late nineteenth century, such as George B. Shaw's *The Quintessence of Ibsenism* (1891), and Leo Tolstoy's *What Is Art* (1898), that elucidate the principles of realism in literature, whether in drama or fiction, and relate them to Chekhov's practice in *The Seagull*.

- Research the structural principles of the "well made" play, that is, one that follows the form described by Aristotle in his discussion of tragedy in *The Poetics*. Compare those principles with Chekhov's practice in *The Seagull*.

- Research Count Leo Tolstoy's complaints about Chekhov's alleged failure to use his art to advance a moral cause. Explain whether or not you think that charge is validated by the playwright's thematic concerns in the play.

Alienation and Loneliness

A theme developed and exploited in much of modern literature is the individual's susceptibility to a sense of isolation and alienation in an environment that is basically inimical to that individual's emotional or mental health. The most important isolated figure in Chekhov's play is Konstantine Treplyov, the uncompromising artist alienated from those around him because they are much too conventional to share his convictions about a need for "new forms." He is, of course, even isolated from his mother, a selfish woman who perceives her son as a rather unpleasant and distressingly gloomy young man who threatens both her pocketbook and those things held most dear to her—her career and her loyalty to Boris Trigorin.

Familial alienation is also found elsewhere in the play. For example, Masha and her mother, Pauline, are both unhappy with Shamreyeff. Masha finds him impossible to confide in and seeks a surrogate father in the person of Dorn, to whom she confesses her love for Konstantine. Her mother, meanwhile, also looks for love from Dorn, a man who seems constitutionally ill-suited to fulfill the needs of either of the two supplicants. Another example is Nina, who is alienated from her father and stepmother, background characters who have a disapproving, puritanical suspicion of their artistic neighbors.

Others, like Sorin, experience a different kind of isolation. Once a magistrate with the authority of law supporting him, he has lost control of his own estate, even of his life. He is estranged from the only life he valued, that of the town, and is simply bored by the country. Dorn and Shamreyeff, even Trigorin, offer parallel examples in their own peculiar way.

Apathy and Passivity

While some of the characters in *The Seagull* struggle with their frustrated desires, a few seem apathetically resigned to living their unfulfilled lives with only a token resistance to their fate. Examples in the play are Dorn and Sorin and to a lesser degree Trigorin. While to some extent these men protest against their fate, they do little or nothing to change it. Sorin is simply bored by his rural life, yet he evidences neither the ambition nor the gumption to alter it, even to take charge of his estate's affairs. Although the town life that he is so nostalgic about is but a short carriage ride away, he just listlessly slides along, unable to muster up the physical or mental energy to return to it. Dorn, despite Pauline's passion for him, seems oddly detached from those around him. He does little or nothing to encourage Pauline. He seems also to have given up the practice of medicine, perhaps because the profession has left him virtually penniless. He seems more a hesitant observer than a doer, even in such simple matters as medicating the ailing Sorin. Even Trigorin, a successful writer, is curiously apathetic about his fame. He would rather spend his time at the estate's lake fishing, away from the company of the other characters, engaging in his private reveries.

These characters help give the play its crepuscular feel, that unnerving sense of lassitude that marks Chekhov's greatest plays. As in the actual Russian society at the time, the people in these plays talk of necessary change but prove ineffectual when it comes to effecting it, drawn as they are into a morass of self-indulgence, languishing in memories of better moments in their lives while life simply slips away from them.

Artists and Society

To some extent, *The Seagull* is concerned with the artist's role in society. Chekhov, who throughout his career had been subjected to criticism for his unwillingness to use his pen for doctrinaire purposes, was profoundly interested in the matter of the writer's social or political responsibilities and obligations. He was also writing at a time when not just the content but also the form and technique of literary works were undergoing revolutionary change.

Through his various characters, Chekhov studies the conflict arising from the resistance of tradition to that change. Clearly, Madame Arkadina, a denizen of the existing theater, embodies the views of the establishment. Standing against her is her own son, Konstantine, who preaches the need for a new art, one of "new forms," an art of forward-looking ideas, not one that merely entertains with timeworn conventions and hackneyed ideas that no longer have any social relevance. As his play indicates, the new art should have prophetic insights into humankind's destiny. His would be a theater light years away from the theater that, for example, Shamreyeff favors, a theater of brick bats and pratfalls.

The conflict in *The Seagull* is only studied, not resolved. Even though Trigorin argues that both the traditional theater and allied literary arts and new ones could coexist, the closemindedness of the adherents to the old and the new argue that such an accommodation can not be. Konstantine's art is dismissed by his unsympathetic mother as the ravings of his "bad temper," while he sees in hers a mindless art that merely continues to pander to the bumptious fools making up the traditional theater audience. Meanwhile, as members of the artistic community spar on these issues, the philistines try to isolate them, dismissing them, as Nina's father and stepmother do, as immoral bohemians.

Love and Passion

The melancholy that pervades *The Seagull* arises from pangs of despised or unrequited love. In Chekhov's intricate design, most characters are both victim and tormentor, loving one of the others while rejecting the love of another character. That is, in the various triangular liaisons, each character loves another who either totally rejects that love or abuses it while having his or her own desires spurned by a third character. Konstantine Treplyov, for example, loves Nina, but she pursues Boris Trigorin, who ends up treating her very badly. Meanwhile, Masha pines after Konstantine, who only views her as a pest. She in turn is loved by Medvedenko, and although she does not love the schoolmaster, marries him as a convenience and then treats him shamelessly. Those not caught up in this sort of triangular love intrigue seem no better off—particularly, of course, Irina Arkadina, a selfish narcissist who is unable to face aging gracefully or find any satisfaction in her maternal role.

Identity: The Search for Self

The principal searcher in *The Seagull* is Konstantine, although in one way or another each of the main characters is trying to find an identity in a relationship that is fated to disappoint them all. Konstantine's quest is artistic. He seeks "new forms," to break with a conventional theater epitomized by his mother, the highly successful actress. Although Konstantine's desire for Nina plays a part in his frustrations, his mother's scoffing dismissal of his work and the acclaim afforded Boris Trigorin, whom he deems unworthy, are also devastating influences. When he finds his own work growing conventional, Treplyov despairs and, rejected again by Nina, shoots himself for a second time.

Other characters are caught in situations that prevent an inner peace or self-fulfilling relationship with another figure. For example, both Masha and her mother, Pauline, look to Dorn to help them alleviate their disquietude, to provide something lacking in their lives. Masha treats him as a surrogate father, confiding her feelings in him, while Pauline, unhappy with her husband, tries to inflame a passion in him for her. Dorn remains too detached, growing passionate only in his approval of Konstantine's artistic efforts to produce his "new forms." Others are similarly frustrated—Sorin, for example, by country life, which he finds tedious, or Trigorin, who seems to find no satisfaction in his success as a writer.

Success and Failure

In *The Seagull,* those who succeed in one sense invariably fail in another. In material terms, the most successful characters are Irina Arkadina and her companion, Boris Trigorin. She is an acclaimed actress, he a renowned writer. Both seem to sacrifice much of their essential decency to their success, however. Fearful of what the loss of beauty might do for her career, Irina is much too self-centered to respond to the needs of her son Konstantine. As a reminder that she is growing old, something that she cannot face, he simply annoys and threatens her. Meanwhile, Trigorin is so jaded by his success that he has grown cynical and desultory. He treats the adoring Nina badly, abandoning her when she badly needs his support.

In the case of Konstantine, a growing success has as an ironic consequence, for the acclaim makes him feel that he has somehow sold out his ideals, that he has failed to bring about the revolutionary change needed to develop "new forms" in writing. His publication of a story in the same magazine that contains one by Boris Trigorin distresses him, and in the play's last act, along with Nina's final rejection, it leads to his depression and second attempt at suicide.

Time

Time is the main enemy in *The Seagull*. In fact, it may be viewed as the play's principal antagonist. It is relentless and erosive, never a healing influence, as it is, for example, in a play like Shakespeare's *Winter's Tale*. Its effect pervades the lives of all the characters, and, because that is basically true to life, it is a defining element of Chekhov's realism.

The most devastating impact of its passage is seen between the third and fourth acts, when two years elapse. Nothing works out for the better, or at least what the various characters believe is the better. Sorin grows older and weaker. Irina Arkadina's beauty continues to fade. Nina's acting career goes nowhere. Perhaps worse yet, other things remain the same. If it is not betrayed, love merely languishes in its hopelessness, molding like some buds that rot without ever bearing fruit. Masha marries her schoolmaster, Semyon Medvedenko, and bears him a child but is neither a loving wife nor mother, still suffering from a misguided passion for Konstantine, who, in turn, still pines for Nina. Time, merely implacable, works to no one's advantage in *The Seagull*.

Aestheticism

The Seagull reflects Chekhov's aesthetic concern with his art. Several of the characters in the play are to some degree interested in the nature and theory of literary and dramatic arts. Two of them, Boris Trigorin and Konstantine Treplyov, are writers, while two others, Irina Arkadina and Nina Zaryechny, are actresses. Others, like Dorn and Shamreyeff, offer critical judgments on these arts. In fact, Sorin's estate serves as a kind of retreat for artists and intellectuals, and much of the play's dialogue, rich with allusions and topical references, concerns artistic matters. From the vantage point of Nina's puritanical father and stepmother, who remain offstage, those who gather there are self-indulgent and immoral. Nina's parent's view reflects the traditional attitudes still dominant in Russia at the time.

Style

Allusion

The Seagull makes use of allusion to literary works that in their suggestiveness enrich the texture of Chekhov's play. Chief among these is Shakespeare's *Hamlet,* from which Konstantine and his mother quote lines that help define their own relationship. Konstantine is angry with his mother for her attachment to Boris Trigorin, a man whom he intensely dislikes, as Hamlet dislikes Claudius. Like Hamlet, too, Konstantine erupts into fury with his mother, though as much for her selfishness as for her attachment to Trigorin. Like *Hamlet, The Seagull* is open to a Freudian, Oedipal interpretation of the relationship between Treplyov and his mother, a view buoyed up by a similar and common reading of the relationship between Hamlet and his mother, Gertrude.

Another allusion in *The Seagull,* concerns a story by the French writer, Guy de Maupassant. De Maupassant one of the very successful exponents of realism in fiction—still a relatively "new form" in Chekhov's day, but one against which contemporary currents were already beginning to turn. There are also several allusions to the Russian theater of the day, some of which provide insights to the characters who make them, though these references are more topical and less memorable than those made to Shakespeare.

Comedy of Manners

The Seagull, though not in mood or theme, has some similarities to a comedy of manners, those amoral drawing-room pieces of the English stage in the eighteenth century. In them, love intrigues are the principal focus of both the dramatists and his characters, and adultery is at least condoned if not actually practiced. Some characters, often libertines, are caught in triangular relationships that impose dilemmas that must be resolved through wit and clever stratagems, even reformation of character. In them, clever young rakes manage to satisfy the heart while also replenishing an empty purse.

Chekhov's comedy is much heavier, of course, and its outcome very different. In *The Seagull,* love's quests are frustrated and triumph over financial adversity remains an unrealized dream. The potential for self-fulfillment of any kind simply erodes as time passes. However, in its way, and certainly compared to much nineteenth-century melodrama, *The Seagull* shares with the earlier comedy of manners a complex intrigue plot, a degree of amorality, a focal concern with social mores, and a setting—a country estate—offering an ideal locale for the various character encounters necessary to the intrigue. As with some of those earlier plays, there is also an apparent shapelessness to *The Seagull.*

Conflict

There is no central conflict in *The Seagull,* no struggle between a protagonist and some opposing character or force, but there are minor conflicts arising from a character's desire out of harmony with the needs or aspirations of another character. Mostly these have to do with love, invariably misplaced in the play. The play chronicles the frustrations of most of the major characters, their fruitless efforts to achieve what they want, and in a few cases—like that of Konstantine—depicts their disillusionment when they manage to gain a measure of success, if not in love, then at least in fortune.

Some of the conflict is familial, pitting offspring against parent, as in the case of Konstantine and his mother, but more often it arises from unrequited love. It leads to unhappiness, to the misery that seems to afflict all but the more dispassionate characters, Dorn, for example, or the waspish Shamreyeff, both of whom are aloof from love. In any case, the conflicts remain unresolved, at best only dimmed or diluted by the passage of time.

Farce

There is a very limited use of the low comic in *The Seagull,* elements of which abound in some of Chekhov's earlier one-act curtain raisers. Still, there are some farcical moments that help remind the audience that the play is, after all, a comedy, and that some of the characters' behavior is a kind of posturing. For example, there is something insincere about Masha's unhappiness expressed in the play's opening dialogue. "I am in mourning for my life," she says, and she wears Hamlet's "inky cloak" as an outward manifestation of her professed inner sorrow, which, at least to Medvedenko, she cannot explain.

How seriously and sympathetically is the audience to take Masha or, for that matter, other unhappy figures, even Konstantine and Nina? *The Seagull* can be interpreted for staging as rather gloomy melodrama, or, as Chekhov himself seems to have wanted, it can be interpreted more as comedy. At times it seems to jar back and forth between the two moods, as, for example, in Konstantine's blundered suicide attempt. Its serious import is comically punctured when, after failing to blow his brains out, he appears with a turban-sized bandage on his head. In reminding the audience that life is not shaped as either comedy or tragedy, Chekhov juxtaposes a mundane observation or event against a soulful outpouring or serious action, and at times uses a kind of comic bathos, pitting the ridiculous against the sublime.

Fin de siècle

In art, *fin de siècle* suggests both art for its own sake and, warranted or not, decadence. The term was used to refer to artists in various genres who were breaking with tradition, producing works that defied conventional morality and eschewed a didactic function. Many of the artists involved led scandalous lives, flaunting that morality in their public behavior, the free-spirited Oscar Wilde, for example. Konstantine, in his quest for "new forms," is cast in that bohemian mold, full of scorn for tradition and ready to tear down Russia's old theatrical edifice with his revolutionary art.

Foil

A common method of illuminating character in drama is through the use of character foils. It is a technique particularly well suited to plays, which are brief and ephemeral experiences when staged. By using sharply contrasting characters, the playwright is able to present each in high relief, making them both more distinct and memorable. In *The Seagull*, Sorin's character, his ineffectualness, is not just a correlative of his age and increasing feebleness, it is highlighted by the insubordination and surliness of his steward, Ilya Shamreyeff. Similarly, Konstantine Treplyov's imaginative but volatile nature is brought into sharper focus because it is seen against the character of Semyon Medvedenko, who, far more stolid and reasonable, never flies into rages. So, too, Irina Arkadina—a woman who protests too much—has a foil in Nina, a younger reflection of herself, one who in her youthful beauty reminds the older actress that her own beauty is fading. Chekhov effectively reveals other characters through such contrasts.

Oedipus Complex

Much has been made of the relationship of Konstantine and his mother, Irina Arkadina. With loose parallels and even allusion to Shakespeare's *Hamlet,* Chekhov develops an angry young man whose dislike of his mother's companion and lover, Boris Trigorin, transcends an artistic jealousy enlivened by his rebellious contempt for the older man's talent. Konstantine simply hates the man, even wants to kill him, a response that suggests more than a mere disgust with Trigorin's success as a writer. Although controversial, the Freudian explanation—a subconscious sexual jealousy—certainly has merit. The Oedipus Complex involves a male's latent love for his mother and corresponding hatred for his father, his rival for his mother's love. That hatred can be displaced, directed at a surrogate figure, especially if, like both Boris Trigorin in Chekhov's play and King Claudius in *Hamlet,* that person takes the father's place in the mother's bed.

Soliloquy

Curiously enough, Chekhov uses the soliloquy, a device that on the face of it seems inimical to realism. The soliloquy had a traditional use in theater. A vocalized monologue, it was used to reveal the inner thoughts and feelings of a character who delivers the speech while alone on stage. Although the speech may be overheard by hidden auditors, as happens in *Hamlet* for example, generally it reveals the character's inner self only to the audience. The realist's objection to the device is based on the idea that people do not normally talk to themselves aloud, unless, perhaps, they are mentally unbalanced. Chekhov makes spare use of the soliloquy, and perhaps, given what happens in the play, deliberately suggests the character's mental and emotional instability in employing it. In act 4, it is Konstantine who, briefly alone, discontentedly mulls over the fact that he is "slipping into routine." This happens just before Nina appears and again rejects his love, leading to the play's perplexing finale, when Konstantine once again shoots himself.

Symbol

The Seagull has, as is suggested by the play's title, a central symbol, the seagull that Konstantine shoots and lays at the feet of Nina in act 2. Although Nina adopts the seagull as a signatory emblem, with a special meaning for her, its import for the play remains both elusive and debatable. There is no simple equation explaining its purpose. In fact, Chekhov seems to include it offhandedly, almost whimsically, as if defying the reader or viewer to find any meaning to it at all. Even Nina at first says that the symbolic meaning of the gull is beyond her understanding. However, symbols are often elusive beasts, talking points with no definitive answers, in part because they can mean different things to different people. What is clear is that Konstantine is a crack shot, bringing down a bird on the wing, suggesting that his attempt at suicide is deliberately bungled, making the attempt seem a mere ploy for sympathy. In any case, Konstantine relates the killing of the bird, a thing of beauty, to his depressed emotional state. He speaks of earlier events, including the failure of his play—which, like the seagull's life—was aborted by an act of cruelty, that is, by his mother's dismissive scorn. He also tells Nina that he has burned the manuscript of his play, deliberately destroying what, in his view, was a thing of beauty.

Other symbols in the play include the estate's lake, which, like the gull, means different things to different characters. Dorn sees it as magical, able to evoke dreams, while Trigorin views it more practically, as a refuge, a place to fish, and Nina as a catalytic influence in her desire to become an actress. Flowers figure in the play, too. In their ephemeral beauty, they suggest the fragile dreams of various characters, which, like the flowers in the play, are deliberately destroyed or succumb to the ravages of time.

Historical Context

In the year in which Chekhov's *The Seagull* was first staged, 1896, Nicholas II, of the Romanov dynasty, became the last czar of Russia, a nation that at the time had a population of about 128 million people. Dominated by the Russian Orthodox Church, an inept bureaucracy, and an entrenched landed and hereditary aristocracy, the vast country had settled into a seemingly inert, twilight period, a sort of fitful hibernation resistant to political change and social amelioration. While many members of the educated class recognized a need for progress, they were largely ineffectual in achieving much of anything until violent revolution brought the Bolsheviks to power in 1917 and Russia, for good or ill, finally entered the modern world. Until then, despite some unrest, including a crushed rebellion in 1906, Russia was simply a sleeping giant that had barely started to respond to the industrial revolution that a century before had begun transforming many of its European neighbors to the west into emerging industrial powers. However, at the same time, despite its backwardness and cultural isolation, Russia produced some of the greatest writers, composers, and artists of the age, among whom Chekhov stands in the front rank. Russian cities, notably Moscow and St. Petersburg, were cultural centers of tremendous importance, and places, too, where new ideas were fomented by a growing number of disaffected intellectuals. But these cities also lacked adequate housing, health care, and transportation and communication facilities, and were plagued by poverty and disease—including tuberculosis, the consumptive sickness which, even as he wrote *The Seagull,* was slowly wasting Chekhov's own life.

Although the modern age in the United States —and such European countries as England, France, and Germany—was dawning more rapidly than in the future Soviet Union, a much accelerated rate of change awaited inventions and discoveries that in 1896 were, at best, still in their infancy. In that year, Henry Ford drove his first car through the streets of Detroit and the German scientist, Wilhelm Roentgen, discovered x-rays. Also, the dial telephone and electric lamp were patented in America, and the first movie was screened in the Netherlands. In that year, too, the first modern Olympic Games opened in Athens, a seminal event that presaged the breakdown in the isolation of nations and the advent of internationalism in the postindustrial age.

Besides changes wrought through science and technology, social and political changes were in the winds. The impact of two major thinkers—Karl Marx and Charles Darwin—continued to affect everything from politics and religion to art and letters. It was in the 1890s that a third major thinker, Sigmund Freud, had begun evolving his psychoanalytical method, providing new and sometimes distressing insights into human behavior. Freud would greatly impact both literature and art, which, in the same era, were already in search of new directions and the "new forms" of which Konstantine speaks in *The Seagull*. The fin de siècle artists of the 1890s, although a hydra-headed group, were united in their efforts to replace the traditional with the new and different, to experiment with form and technique. Although never given to the personal excesses of many of his contemporaries, Chekhov, particularly in his last few plays, reflects that need to make things new.

Critical Overview

Anton Chekhov wrote *The Seagull* in 1895, at the demarcation point between his first and second periods of development as a dramatist. In the first stage, starting in 1881, the writer was chiefly recognized for his adaptations of his own short fiction into "vaudevilles," one-act farces that were very popular curtain raisers in Russian theater. To a great extent, these are formulaic pieces, focusing on the absurdities of such eccentric character types as the hypochondriacal suitor and his man-desperate, bride-to-be counterpart in *The Marriage Proposal* (1888-1889) or the blustering male intruder and the reclusive, long-suffering widow in *The Bear* (1888).

Compare & Contrast

- **1890s:** Long travel is difficult, limited principally to rail and horseback or horse-drawn cart, carriage, or sleigh, often on roads that for half the year were impassable. Although the telephone has come into use in some cities in Europe and America, it has not yet reached the likes of Sorin's country estate. While such estates could be situated fairly close to towns providing railway connections to Moscow and other major cities, many people live their lives never venturing more than a few miles away from where they were born.

Today: Modern technology makes it possible for even the most physically isolated communities to stay in touch, not just with the world's urban centers, but with each other. Today, even those geographically isolated in what few wilderness outposts remain, or in transit over the world's remote regions, can talk to relatives or friends with whom a reunion may be just a few hours or, at most, a day or two away.

- **1890s:** Medicine, though verging on important breakthroughs, is a dreadfully imperfect art. There is little understanding of the nature of most diseases, of the bacteria or viruses that caused them, thus treatment is largely limited to dealing with the symptoms rather than the causes. Medicine is also unregulated, and many doctors, some of them quacks, depend upon homeopathy and herbal-based, family elixirs, passed down from one generation to another. Alcohol and opium derivatives are standard painkillers, dispensed without much knowledge of their addictive nature.

All too often, patients are sent to hospitals, not to be cured, but to die. By the end of the nineteenth century, average life-expectancy in the United States is in the mid-forties. In Russia it is even lower.

Today: Medicine may still be an imperfect art, but scientific advances in the twentieth century have made it a much more exact and effective one. More medicinal practises are preventative in nature. Through immunization, doctors control diseases that used to be dreaded killers. Physicians and medical scientists now attempt to discover the cause of a sickness, for if the cause can be isolated, a cure is deemed possible. That life expectancy will soon double that of a century ago is evidence of the great strides medicine has made in the last one hundred years.

- **1890s:** Aside from the entertainment provided by books and card and board games, most home entertainment has to be provided "in-house" by those dwelling or visiting there. The houses of the upper and middle classes usually have pianos and other musical instruments; some even have music rooms, where family members can gather to form small chamber-music ensembles. Plays and recitations were common, too. There is, in fact, a fairly active engagement of family members and guests in the production of entertainment.

Today: Thanks to great technological advances, family members and guests can enjoy a tremendous array of entertainment experiences simply by "channel surfing" on television or the Internet, or by inserting different compact discs or tapes in home-entertainment components. In fact, the greatest audience for various arts is now found in the home, not at the live event. The home audience is more passive now, however, and often has no participatory role in providing entertainment.

- **1890s:** Class distinctions are still strongly etched in the consciousness of its citizens, even though the serfs have been liberated for several years and a middle class is rapidly emerging.

Today: Although in many democratic societies there remains a vestigial sense of class distinctions, power associated with class and hereditary right has greatly diminished. Class distinctions today are usually based on wealth, education level, or professional standing, and they are reflected more in such things as country-club memberships and cultural tastes than in the size of one's estate and the number of servants in the household.

Also belonging to the first period are four full-length plays, two of which are no longer extant. In only one of these, *The Wood Demon* (1889), did the playwright begin experimenting with an "indirect action" technique in an attempt to more faithfully represent actual life, free of the many stage conventions that, because they in some way falsified it, had become anathema to realists. However, until entering his second period with *The Seagull,* Chekhov still continued to depend on traditional techniques and devices, including direct, on-stage action and plots contrived to heighten dramatic impact and force an artificial closure.

In the inner-action technique used in *The Seagull,* some of the most vital action occurs offstage, not just Konstantine's two attempts at suicide, but in events that transpire between acts, as, for example, the ill-fated liaison of Trigorin and Nina and the unfortunate marriage of Masha and Medvedenko. Most of these events occur between acts 3 and 4, when two years pass. Furthermore, on the surface, *The Seagull* totally lacks the causal arrangement of episodes that characterized the more traditional fare of the time. Since action is not locked together in a discernible pattern, the work seems almost shapeless, much like life itself.

These daring departures from the usual theatrical fare were simply too much for the St. Petersburg audience when the play premiered there on October 17, 1896. It was staged at the Alexandrinsky Theater, a house that was, as quoted in Lantz, "associated with popular, low-brow entertainment," and was turned into "a complete fiasco," in part because it was "an inadequate production that was unequal to the play's striking dramatic innovations." In fact, as quoted in Styan, the Alexandrinsky's own literary committee forewarned that the play's structure was too loose and carped about its "symbolism, or more correctly its Ibsenism." In any case, the play was hastily prepared for production under the direction of E. M. Karpov, a writer of popular melodramas who evidenced little sympathy for Chekhov's revolutionary technique, and when it went on the boards, it was openly mocked. The reaction devastated the playwright, who left the Alexandrinsky confused and deeply depressed. Although audiences for the remaining performances in the eight-day run were more receptive, the damage to the dramatist had already been done.

One of the harshest critics of the play was Leo Tolstoy, who, in 1897, voiced his wholly unfavorable opinions to Chekhov's close friend, Alezxy Suvorin. As David Magarshack notes, while admitting that *The Seagull* was "chock full of all sorts of things," Tolstoy complained that nobody had an inkling of what they were there for, and he dismissed the work as "a very bad play." That was a view shared by many, most of whom were blind-sided by Chekhov's innovative genius. As Magarshack notes, "apart from his purely moral objections to Chekhov's characters, Tolstoy's main criticisms of Chekhov's plays concern their structure and their apparent lack of purpose."

Fortunately, both for Chekhov and the modern theater, a complete reversal in the play's fortunes occurred in 1898, two years after the initial staging, when the newly formed Moscow Art Theatre revived it under the joint direction of that group's founders, Vladimir Nemirovich-Danchenko and Konstantin Stanislavsky. These two, brilliant advocates of ensemble theater, were dedicated to purging the Russian theater of its insidious star system, in which plays, often bad, were written as vehicles for popular actors. They were also dedicated to preserving the authority of the dramatist, to honoring a play's text and its creator's intentions.

Nemirovich-Danchenko, who knew Chekhov, convinced both the reluctant dramatist and Stanislavsky to attempt a revival of *The Seagull* at the Moscow Art Theatre. After a rigorous rehearsal schedule, it opened there on December 17, 1898, and was greeted with tremendous enthusiasm and deafening applause. Although the work was not the first play produced by the M.A.T., it was the one that brought it overnight fame, and it acknowledged its indebtedness to the play by adopting a seagull as its own symbol.

The play also brought critical acclaim for Chekhov, who thereafter was inspired to continue writing for the stage, producing three other masterpieces before his untimely death in 1904. Although some, like Irina Kirk, view the work as "the most innovative of his plays," the other three that came in its wake—*Uncle Vanya, Three Sisters,* and *The Cherry Orchard*—are generally more highly regarded, and in the history of theater have been more frequently revived. Some modern criticism views *The Seagull,* if not as a mediocre play, at least a flawed one. Echoes of the original complaints about the play's loose structure and blatant symbolism persist. Still, as the first of the four major plays, *The Seagull* enjoys a reputation both for being Chekhov's seminal work in his second and greatest period of writing for the stage and a fascinating play in its own right.

What Do I Read Next?

- August Strindberg's *Miss Julie* (1888) and its "Foreword," in which the dramatist reveals the Darwinian influence on his art, is worth contrasting with Chekhov's themes and technique in *The Seagull*.

- Henrik Ibsen's *Hedda Gabler* (1890) is also worth comparing with *The Seagull* for its themes and technique. One early complaint with Chekhov's play was that it evidenced too strong an influence of Ibsen.

- Maxim Gorky's play, *The Lower Depths* (1902), a more naturalistic play than any by Chekhov, focuses on lower-class Russians struggling for survival. Like Chekhov, Gorky came to prominence through productions at the Moscow Art Theatre.

- *Anna Karenina* (1875-1877), by Leo Tolstoy, is one of the greatest of all Russian novels. Tolstoy, though he wrote plays, is really only remembered for his fiction. He had a tremendous influence on Chekhov.

- *Heartbreak House* (1916), by George Bernard Shaw, has some interesting parallels to Chekhov's play. Its focal interest is the eroding of class distinctions, also of concern to Chekhov. Shaw's play also takes place in a country house, that of Hesione Hushabye. Like Sorin's estate, it provides a microcosmic setting for investigating a social hierarchy.

- *The Autumn Garden* (1951), by Lillian Hellman, reflects Chekhov's influence in its technique, structure, and theme. Generations of family and friends gather together, haplessly trying to reinvigorate their lives, which have settled into dull and listless routines.

Sources

Auden, W. H., "Musee des Beaux Arts," in *The Norton Anthology of English Literature,* Vol. 2, edited by M. H. Abrams, 5th ed., W. W. Norton & Company, 1985, p. 2298.

Caputi, Anthony, *Eight Modern Plays,* Norton, 1991, p. 133.

Chekhov, Anton, *Anton Chekhov: A Life,* by Donald Rayfield, Henry Holt, 1997, p. 353.

Karlinsky, Simon, "The Seagull," in *Letters of Anton Chekhov,* translated by Michael Henry Heim, Harper & Row, 1973, p. 280.

Kirk, Irina, *Anton Chekhov,* Twayne Publishers, 1981, p. 133.

Lantz, K. A., *Anton Chekhov: A Reference Guide to Literature,* G. K. Hall & Co., 1985, p. xix.

Magarshack, David, *Chekhov the Dramatist,* Hill and Wang, 1960, pp. 17, 159-160, 163-164.

———, *The Seagull,* Barnes & Noble, 1972, pp. 21-23.

Moravcevich, Nicholas, "Chekhov and Naturalism: From Affinity to Divergence," in *Anton Chekhov's Plays,* edited by Eugene K. Bristow, Norton, 1977, pp. 294-295.

Styan, J. L., *Chekhov in Performance: A Commentary on the Major Plays,* Cambridge

University Press, 1971, pp. 10, 13.

Valency, Maurice, "The Sea Gull," in *The Breaking String: The Plays of Anton Chekhov,* Oxford, 1966, p. 154.

Further Reading

Hahn, Beverly, *Chekhov: A Study of the Major Stories and Plays,* Cambridge University Press, 1977.

> Although in drama Hahn's principal focus is on *The Cherry Orchard,* her refutation of the dramatist's alleged deficiencies—for example his formlessness, insipidity, and negativism—is very helpful for understanding Chekhov's achievement in his late plays.

Kirk, Irina, *Anton Chekhov,* Twayne Publishers, 1981.

> This overview of Chekhov and his work offers a good starting point for further study. It offers brief but insightful interpretations of Chekhov's plays and the artistic principles underlying them.

Lantz, K. A., *Anton Chekhov: A Reference Guide to Literature,* G. K. Hall, 1985.

> For those needing to conduct further research on Chekhov, this is an indispensable aid. It includes a biography and checklist of the author's works with both English and Russian titles, with a helpful

annotated bibliography of critical studies published before 1984.

Magarshack, David, *Chekhov the Dramatist,* Hill and Wang, 1960.

> In this introduction to Chekhov's plays, Magarshack divides the dramatist's canon into "plays of direct action" and "plays of indirect action," with *The Wood Demon* serving as a transitional work between the two types. He relates *The Seagull* to Chekhov's life and his estate in Melikhovo.

———, *The Real Chekhov: An Introduction to Chekhov's Last Plays,* Allen & Unwin, 1972.

> This study offers a scene by scene analysis of each of Chekhov's four major plays and the dramatist's attitude towards matters addressed in them-which, in the case of *The Seagull,* Magarshack argues, is the nature of art.

Styan, J. L., *Chekhov in Performance: A Commentary on the Major Plays,* Cambridge University Press, 1971.

> Styan also provides a close analysis of Chekhov's four major plays. A principal focus is the "submerged life" of the playwright's text and Chekhov's stage technique. Styan

also discusses the preparation and initial staging of each play.

Valency, Maurice, *The Breaking String: The Plays of Anton Chekhov,* Oxford University Press, 1966.

This work relates Chekhov's major plays both to his own fiction and to the Russian theater of his day. Valency argues that Chekhov is essentially an ironist and comedist, although each play involves the breaking of a "golden string" that binds man both to his heavenly father and his own past.

Williams, Lee J., *Anton Chekhov, the Iconoclast,* University of Scranton Press, 1989.

This study takes the view that Chekhov was a self-conscious agent of change in Russia, that he employed a scientific method to dispel old, class-biased myths about Russian peasants, and that in both method and philosophy he was, as the title indicates, a dedicated iconoclast.